# THE PRESIDENT NEXT DOOR

poems, songs, and journalism

## Philip Martin

et alia
press

Little Rock, Arkansas
2015

Published in the United States of America by:
Et Alia Press
1819 Shadow Lane
Little Rock, AR 72207

etaliapress.com


ISBN: 817525766-0
Library of Congress Control Number:




Edited by Erin Wood.
Layout design by Kathy Oliverio.
Cover design by Jesse Nickles.

The following poems and song lyrics are unpublished with the following exceptions:

A different poem titled "Matty Alou" appeared in The Giant Bee Journal in 1993. "The Pry Bar" appears in *Scars: An Anthology* (Et Alia Press, 2015). A prose version of "Bad Brain" appeared in Volume 1 of the *Arkansas Literary Forum*, an online literary journal, in 1999. A draft of "September Morning, 2001" appeared in Volume 6: 2004, of the *Arkansas Literary Forum*. "Ray Chapman, Killed by Pitch August 16, 1920," a finalist for the 2013 James Hearst Poetry Prize, appeared in the Spring 2013 issue of *North American Review*. A draft of "September Morning, 2001" appeared in Volume 6: 2004, of the *Arkansas Literary Forum*.

The songs "Brother Bob," "Cassius Clay," "Closest Friend" and "Gastonia" appear on the 2013 album *Gastonia* (Strangepup Records). The songs "Bill Clinton," "Euclid Avenue," "Stand My Ground," "Thomas Chatterton" and "Urban Shocker" appear on the 2014 album *Euclid Avenue* (Strangepup Records).

For Karen, my closest friend

# TABLE OF CONTENTS

# Author's Note

I have worked in newspapers—as a reporter, editor, columnist and critic—my entire adult life.

I have also written—and sometimes performed—songs since I was 12 or 13 years old. I read somewhere that Lou Reed, that student of Delmore Schwartz, had, before he became famous, published some of his song lyrics as poetry in little magazines. That delighted me, and gave me ideas.

I tried to write poetry when I was young, but gave it up when I found it too hard to approach my models. I only began trying to write more than doggerel about a decade ago, when I was encouraged by two great writers—two great men. Donald Harington told me I should suspend my modesty when I set out to write, that I should shout over all those voices I thought sweeter and stronger than my own. He thought it was worth me trying, and without his confidence I doubt I would have.

Miller Williams worked with me on specific poems, talked to me about theory, about lying my way to the truth and the sacredness of necessary honesty. He also published my books of essays, and became more like family than mentor to me.

I wish those men were alive to hold this volume in their hands.

It is a collection of song lyrics and poems, more than a few of which were inspired by my work for newspapers. I should hope there is truth in all of them, though I don't know if they would withstand a thorough fact-checking.

I also have some people I must thank, chief among them the generous poet Johnny Wink, who read—and often improved—these poems. Johnny gave me copious feedback and led me to slaughter a few pernicious darlings. I also want to express my appreciation to several editors who shaped me as journalist and writer— Griffin Smith, Michael Lacey, Stan Tiner, Stephen Buel, Jack Schnedler and Suzy Smith.

And Erin Wood, my editor at Et Alia Press, was a kind, observant and patient partner in the process of producing this book.

Finally, I wish to tell my wife, closest friend, most critical reader and first-last-best editor Karen Martin that I love her and our life together. She's the best.

## TALIESIN DESTROYED BY FIRE:
## EDWIN CHENEY SPEAKS TO FRANK LLOYD WRIGHT IN A
## CLUB CAR, TRAVELING TO CLAIM THE BODIES

What is it, Frank, but
a numb muscle in my chest?
I want to make it into
a pain,
aciculate and memorable.
Yet it is simply
and undeniably
a dull organ,
my heart.

You tell me, Frank,
my wife is dead.
My children too.
It has devastated you.
I see.

I do not blame you
for loving her or her
for loving you or you
for hiring or allowing to be hired
that madman cook
from the islands.

None of that could be helped.
Pascal says,
"Love has reasons that reason cannot know."
Right?

I was privileged to be your client.
You are a genius
and I understand
that those whom the gods so favor
should not be bound
by the petty circumscription of man's society
or shamed by the tuneless grief
of an electrical engineer.

# EUCLID AVENUE

## (a ballad in A minor)

On the train from Chicago to Wisconsin,
Edwin Cheney said to Frank Lloyd Wright:
Maestro, my heart is a numb muscle,
a dull pump bumping blackly in the night.
They tell me death is but an illusion,
and we are made of naught but bone and spit.
I know this world's a lousy contract,
I haven't got the wherewithal to quit.
So I'll accompany you to Taliesin
to poke through the cooled ruins of my life.
There I'll collect the corpses of my children
and leave you with the body of my wife.

"To live outside the law, you must be honest."
I have heard these words attributed to you.
You lit out on your spiritual Hegira
and abandoned me to Euclid Avenue.

I know, Frank, that you are a great artist,
due all the things your genius can command
So I will stand beside you on the platform
and before I leave, I'll smile and shake your hand
For laws and rules are made for dull men,
not for the brave and spiritually austere.
I know I was privileged just to be your client;
I've paid your fee, now I'll disappear.
For laws and rules are made for dull men,
not for the brave and spiritually austere.
One can't expect the angels to attend to
the tuneless grief of some bald engineer.

# HERMANN KAFKA AT THE GRAVESIDE OF HIS SON

I am the respectable villain;
conventional and much concerned
with the illusion of security
my place and family provide me.

You are the dead, ingracious hero
wild and reproachful even as the dirt
(I've paid for) rattles on your coffin,
and immortality swallows you.

I was the schocet's son; I was poor.
I had no time for pimps or poetry
yet I allowed you your leisure and
I was not so coarse not to take pride
in the glories that accrued to you.
You thought me too dull to recognize
the steepled ruins of Palestine or
the pain inflicted by breath and bowel.

I look on this Dora, this banshee,
who calls her suffering evidence
of a love too great for men like me
to parse. On me your fineness wasted,
like a silk robe on an Iroquois.

I stand here in black wool and take it;
Pocket jangling coins, waiting for night
to overtake all philosophy
and deliver us to nothingness.
This is my prayer; common and low,
unmumbled, unscreamed, but felt
pith deep in my bourgeois belly:
I'll never mourn for you, my son.
I know that you're the lucky one.

# For a rabbit

Terrier sisters caught the scent;
flushed the rabbit from the deck.
In calm horror I watched as he went
across the yard and doubled back—
crazy scutted and hell-bent—
our girls pursuing, tan and black.
The chase—their feral sacrament.

He would, I thought (hoped) get away
as wild critters often will.
But on this green dappled day
Paris and Dublin scored a kill.

Who, in plastic, wrapped him up
and dropped him in the garbage can?
Who spoke kind words to bereft pets,
who searched his face for their command?

Who gives the animals their names
and manufactures hate and fear?
The fellow who sits at this desk
and scratches at a proffered ear.

I love them beyond reasoning
though I'll never understand
the mind that murderously compels
the little dogs beneath my hands.

# THE WITNESSES

Before the snap, I felt the air, I swear,
go sour, and the hair rise on my neck.
Atoms, or molecules, whatever,
rowing into line. I checked the clock
on the microwave. The time is branded
on my brain—at three thirty three pee em
the transformer blew. I went outside.

The sky was wide, empty, and bluer than
the rime-locked heart of an ancient iceberg.

"Is your power out too?" my neighbor asked.
"It is," I said, "second time this week.
With no weather either; seem strange to you?"
We stood together for a moment, then
we heard the wail and whoop; the sirens sing
and tasted blood and copper in our mouths —
Remembering the scaffolding.

For two weeks or maybe three, we'd seen
them working on the house at Martin Street
and H. They had but got it in the dry
a day or two before; we were impressed
with their industry. They worked together
with uncommon grace and we gathered from
their calm clear faces a joy in making
a thing that would perhaps outlive us all.

We walked toward the construction site
with dread pooling viscous in our bowels.
"Mexicans," she whispered from her porch.
"Their ladder hit the power line. Boom.
Two dead, the other fled in a panic.
I saw the bodies smoking in the street.
They hit a power line. I called the cops."
Just then the van from Channel Four pulled up.

In my life there have been enough bodies,
inert and waxen, their souls scooped out
for me to think there's some electricity
that hums through us a while. And is us.
Or at least is more us than bones and meat
and prayers mumbled in shock and disbelief
over scorched corpses in our quiet street.

If that is so we'll be released one day
though to what mystery I cannot say
and if it's not, then what we build must stand
as circumstantial evidence of man.

# FOR MAYA ANGELOU

We were the people, they the whitefolk.
Their world verged on ours without touching.
I looked on them as wraiths parading,
unclutchable and unreal spirits
gliding pretty with their eerie ways.

Born without grandeur, I was misused
and the devastating clarity
of my voice so thrilled and frightened
I was struck dumb in Arkansas
in communion with the ancient ghosts

who walked through books.

Your life comes at you hard—unbidden
and rampant. And you look up and see
a raw sun or a cold moon climbing
and know the turning, sliding Earth
will one day fall away, delivering

us to the peace of nothingness

or to the bliss in everything.

And so this caged bird dared to sing.

# GODFATHER

## (a blues for Miller Williams)

Vito Corleone was in the hospital
on the first night of 2015.
While my phone was buzzing in the other room,
I focused my attention on the screen.

I watched until they blew up Apollonia
then I took a break and I saw the missed call.
My hands were shaking as I punched the number out
then the world cracked open bitter and banal.

There are times you want to burn down hospitals
and there are times you want to curse at nuns.
These days these times come at briefer intervals:
I hate the gods of cancer, rape, and guns.

Michael Corleone had been exiled to Sicily
when the news came down from Fayetteville.
I sat down at the table and I tried to write
But I ended up taking a sleeping pill.

There are times you want to wreck the universe,
rip out the cosmic ganglia and dreck.
Rage, rage against the doctors and philosophers,
and wear the viscera around your neck.

Godfather, you were such a gentle soul
calm and temperate, courtly as a squire.
I know there'll come a time when I regain control
I know there'll come a time when I expire.

But I've got no pretty words to make it seem all right
I've no breath to waste on sweet clichés.
I know they'll never be another New Year's night
When I don't fondly think upon your ways.

## THE IDIOT HUSBAND TRIES TO TALK HIS WAY OUT OF IT

Miller Williams told me John Ciardi told him
sometimes you have to lie your way to the truth.

That's good to know.
And even better
to remember,
at times like these,
sweetheart.

# BLUES FOR DAEDALUS
## (a country shuffle in G)

Minos held you as a prize
for your ingenuity.
But noble minds will not be tamed;
you longed to be free.
The king had covered all the ports,
he put out an APB.
Someone'd collect a large reward
if he caught you trying to flee.

You looked up into the skies
and devised your crazy scheme.
The more it rolled around your brain,
the more plausible it seemed.
So you photographed the birds
and microscoped a feather.
You worked late nights, built prototypes,
kept one eye on the weather.

You tricked yourself into believing
and found somehow you could.
You never knew how far you flew
but you knew it felt damn good.
You told your kid Icarus,
you had it figured out.
"Crashin' ain't inevitable
if you clear your mind of doubt.
We can ride on battered air,
it's tricky—but achievable."
Then you showed the boy the wings.
He said, "That's cool, Da. Unbelievable."

You sensed he might be overeager,
but you hoped Ick'd be all right.
You regretted there was no time
for a final shakedown flight.
You warned him not to fly too high
not to get above his raisin'
but sons are born to disappoint.
Still, at first it was amazin'.
He did a little loop de loop,
he was poetry in motion,

he climbed into a power stall
—and fell into the ocean.

Heartwrecked you were, but you pushed on
across the blazing sea
to the unblemished beaches
of the isle of Sicily.
And there you built a temple,
walls trued up good and straight,
an Apollonian structure
born of mourning and regret.
You hung your wings there on the wall,
as an offering to the gods,
who'd carried you across the sea
against enormous odds.

But you would never fly again.
You couldn't—not with a heart of lead.
You took some comfort in your work
but some nights you'd lie in bed
and stare through the ceiling
to the silver-peppered sky
from which your son was torn
and try to reason why
he was such a stubborn boy.
You'd wonder if he felt inside
a final jolt of panic or of joy—
and could you call it suicide?

For Ick was Dionysian,
like Rimbaud and Mojo Jim,
like P.B. Shelley and V. Woolf—
was there something wrong with him?
Some imbalance in the brain?
Too much chaos in the heart?
No, it was just an accident.
The kid was brilliant—just not smart.
He had to push the envelope,
he simply had to improvise.
He wasn't strong on fundamentals,
he was gifted, but unwise.

You have always been a careful man.
"Boring" is the term you've heard.

You measured twice for every cut,
and vetted every word
you put down on paper
for somebody else to see.
Maybe you've felt envy for the ones
to whom things come so easily?

Some flash across the firmament
like comets in the sky.
Others worry the least increment;
they draft and test and try
and fail and fail and fail again.
Maybe you lacked the style of Icarus,
but you showed him how to fly.

Maybe it's only wishfulness,
to imagine artists who
don't crack up as a pretty corpse
but work when there is work to do
and attend to dull and picky things
(such as the wax that fixes wings).

# Killer of the assassin Booth, Boston Corbett dies, alone and forgotten, in the Great Hinckley Fire of 1894

Hell hath overtaken me at last.
A world divided, tinder and ash,
limbs lopped from the pines have made a pyre
and now the very air has come afire.
In this ascendant inferno bright
soon I become an angel of light.

I have seen nails coagulated;
massed in their barrels. Glory to God,
I shall not stoop in the boiling creek
this day to save myself a second more
of this impoverished earthly realm.
Oh Lord-er, home I come.

London-born, I was delivered here
to these proud shores. It was in Boston
I was born to Christ. I took the name
and shouted in halls and on the docks;
and in the Fulton Street meetings,
I was called "The Glory to God Man."

Other names they had for me as well:
"The Little Sergeant," "The Mad Hatter,"
(quicksilver vapor gave me the shakes)
"The Avenger of our Fallen Saint."
My head was clear. I raised my rifle.

T'was Providence instructed me—
he raised his carbine and meant to use it on the boys.
Detectives meant to burn him out,
but Doherty was paralyzed.
I acted. Were there orders not to fire?
I heard them not, attending as I was
to the supreme sublime music
of a Higher Authority.

And Stanton, in the end, agreed.
"The rebel is dead—the patriot lives."
And is it not made plain? My bullet
traced the same path as the actor's did
through Old Abraham's spine and head—
does that not proclaim direction
by the divine? It was His hand
that shot John Wilkes Booth dead.

("Useless, useless," he whimpered at the end,
    as Satan reached out a cold and claiming paw.)

I took my money and minor fame
that fed me for some years.
My needs are few, reduced somewhat
by actions rash but necessary.
It takes mettle to follow the law
and if thine own eye offend thee
you are to pluck it out or risk
His wrath. I made myself an eunuch
with a shears to stop the callings
of Satan, fusing from my groin.
I ate in peace a heavy meal
and went to a prayer meeting
before the doctor stitched me up.

I always knew and never shirked
what duties were laid out for me.
After Sumter, I enlisted—
three times in all. I killed seven
Mosby's Rangers before they got me.
They would have shot me down had not
the Gray Ghost himself not seen in my eyes
a hard and holy glint. Instead, he sent
me on to Andersonville.

Where God was good to me.
He spared my life then, only one other
from the fourteen brought in by Mosby.
My example, my prayer-ers,
brought a score more into His hands.
Even the rebel captain asked
for my prayers, and my forgiveness.
He shook my hand, when I was exchanged.

Booth was never a soldier like me.
He was a secesh spy, a coward.
*Booth went up to Charles Town*
*Costumed as a Richmond Gray*
*To see them hang Old John Brown*
*To see the martyr sway.*

*But Brown was serene and Heaven-bound*
*When away the trap door fell*
*Booth barely kept his breakfast down*
*For he caught the stench of Hell.*

*As the angels lifted up John Brown*
*And the slavers cheered and cried*
*And the Devil drove his dray around*
*To give John Booth a ride.*

Booth, they say, was handsome—and vain.
By the scaffold he posed, and in him
I fear was seeded some vile hope
of infamy, and warped glory.
I know not but what I saw—
I heard infernal falsity
in his pretty mocking voice and saw
the devil dancing in his eyes.

In my way, I obliged him of his wish
to die like a soldier. In Garrett's barn,
I was the retributive angel.

(And so now fire engulfs this world;
where is the man with nerve and mercy
enough to deliver me from this?
I will not use my pistol on myself.)

After I killed him there were, of course,
crowds and even women who would have
cared for me, and cooked my supper.
But with admirers came the cranks
and Satan sent 'round Booth's ghost
to murder me. Having dispatched him once
I feared neither specter nor
his Secret Order of his avengers,
though ever-prudent I slept with pistol
by my bed and never walked the streets

without my guns on either hip
and sometimes a shotgun besides.
I preached in New Jersey for a time,
but the clamor was too much for me.
So I went West, to win more souls,
to Bloody Kansas, and in the dust
I dug a home outside Concordia.

As an honest man, my name was known.
I preached some, when invited, but
I kept mainly to myself, distrusting
the motives of the milling mob.
His word I yet preached; Base ball
is a profane game, it despoils
the Sabbath. I will not have it.

I wore my guns for all to see—
those who bear false witness will know
how it feels to have a weapon leveled
at their breast. They dropped the charges
Hallelujah, and, in 1887,
made me assistant doorkeeper
at the Topeka Capitol.

As always, it was duty first—
I went 'round for the heretics,
the police were called to subdue me.
They took me before the probate judge
and dragged me to the asylum,
Andersonville redux. I prayed

and my Lord put a pony in my way.
I helped myself and rode to Thatcher
in Neodesha; I knew him
from the prison camp. A good man,
with a wife I did not much trust.
I left the horse with the livery
(no thief am I) with instructions
for them to contact the asylum
a day or two hence. To Thatcher's wife
I murmured "Mexico," not quite a lie,
I might have gone.

His hand guided me
to these woods.
And though I flew so far, so north, so fast
Hell hath overtaken me at last.
And now, sap pops and great pines crack
the world caves into ashes, smoke is black.
Abba, let this cup of anguish pass from me,
if that be Your will. If not, let it be.

# The Boy Martyr of the Confederacy Spends His Last Night on Earth Defiant

"During the Civil War, seventeen-year-old David Owen Dodd of Little Rock (Pulaski County) was hanged as a spy by the Union army. He has been called the "boy hero of Arkansas" as well "boy martyr of the Confederacy." His story has inspired tributes such as the epic poem "The Long, Long Thoughts of Youth" by Marie Erwin Ward, a full-length play, and reportedly even a 1915 silent Hollywood movie, which has not survived. Historical markers, monuments, annual reenactments of his execution, and the naming of the David O. Dodd Elementary School in southwest Little Rock are among the state's recognitions of his life and death."

— Nancy Hendricks, in the online Encyclopedia of Arkansas[1]


The moon tonight is bright and mean
—a skull hung in the sky.
If you're a man at seventeen
you're not afraid to die.

My stars are wheeling into sync
so I'll tell you the truth:
I never was the sort to think
the long, long thoughts of youth.

Fagan asked for a report
and I tried to oblige.
Like my lawyer kindly told the court
I never did disguise.

who I was or what I did
or where my allegiance lies.
I may be just a stubborn kid.
I know what they do to spies.

Still, it's funny how these glyphs and jots
seem to over matter.
One could play connect the dots
with the soldiers' idle chatter.

---

[1]     encyclopediaofarkansas.net/

Mary Dodge is just a silly flirt,
a mild infatuation.
I'm sorry if her feelings hurt,
but she gave me no information.

I have no hope for an appeal,
no dreams of clemency.
When the ladies went to General Steele—
well, it just embarrassed me.

This college was a jolly place
I wish I'd never left;
Tomorrow I'll wear my brave face
while they strangle me to death.

Our Cause is lost, and so am I.
So is the Confederacy.
To be a martyr one must die
but they'll name a school for me.

The moon tonight is bright and mean
a tin of paraffin.
If you're not grown up at seventeen
you'll never be a man.

# THE FIREMAN

(Over the years I have spoken to many men who have killed women.
The fireman was one who was never convicted.)

With his consciousness awaking,
his soul a roulette pill,
the fireman felt her shaking
and bade her to lie still.

As he looked down from the ceiling
of her seedy double wide
he could surely feel her feeling
the ebb of his salty tide.

He couldn't bear her smirking
at his pitiable scene.
So when she finished jerking,
he wrapped her in Visqueen.

It is sheerest, merest hearsay.
These are things we ought not guess.
But I know the fireman's grim way,
and the horror it suggests.

Men murder when they're slighted,
either think they've been, or are,
then sit up at night, benighted
to plot revenge and war.

# DADDYHYMN

You be the light and the hope
the ramrod assbust crackerheart hope
the whiteface tennishair runningback
the benchmark ballcatcher summamabitch
the homerunning gunnyarmed calling the pitch

This is the way son
Sunhot climbin the stadium
Lift the weight and bang the dumb
cheerleader cunny and comeyhome cum
Make proud the animal crowd
Make the name loud

Do what I tell you
You be the revenue

You be the one, boy
You got the good toy
You got my good genes
Here come the magazines
Sniffjock rollbock
Gloryshock
Tickatock.

Tickatock.

# COPES REYNOLDS, THE SMALL FORWARD

They named me for a bachelor,
to echo his dying line.
It was the way my family had
to honor and to disincline
us from ever bringing shame
on family or given name.

So Cutler and Wellborn and I,
each with our share in Reynolds blood,
were expected to high achieve
and do our best to do good.
Father ran the medical school.
Mother expected that she would
see us follow in his line.
It took with them but not with me.

I liked my school okay, I guess,
except for math and chemistry
and other things a little less . . .
But I loved the squeak my sneakers made.
And the locker room's sweet tang,
the maleness and the Gatorade.
I only did the best I could.

(I rose up—not high, but higher
than they thought the white boy would.
I kept my breath slow and even,
my arms soft, hands softer yet
the ball came off my fingertips
yearning for the nylon net.)

I can recall the mystery
Suspended, hanging, outside time
Which slowed and turned and let me see
The angles and trajectory.
I can't explain—I shot it well.
The paper did a piece on me.
I relaxed into local fame.

I knew my limits more than most

I couldn't play the black boys' game
I wasn't strong or quick enough.
But still I had the golden name
which was enough for LSU
to posit me a Maravich
and invite me to walk on there.

But I languished on the bench
and drank whiskey in Tiger Town.
My grades were poor and finally ...
I let my lovely family down.
It was not quite the end of me.
I tended bar in Vieux Carre.
I played piano in a band.

One night the police took me home
and my brothers made me understand.
I shaved, and cut my hippie hair.
I bought myself a poplin suit
and sat down in a straight-backed chair
before the city editor.
And I answered all his questions.

So now I am a journalist.
A menial profession.
I talk to folks, note what they say
then I type up their confession.
There's time to drink and circulate
And the paycheck is a blessing
bestowed upon a proper fool.

But it's not what they'd have for me,
they think I should go to law school.
I must not love my family —
I'd rather hang out at the Y
or with my buddies at the courthouse.

Don't pin to me your fondest hopes
I'm not Doc Reynolds — I'm just Copes.

# CASSIUS CLAY

## (a folk song in bright G)

My father was a middleweight;
I never saw him fight
still he showed me how to throw a jab
and combo with my right.
He'd cup my head in his hand,
scrape his beard against my cheek—
he was whiskey and Old Spice
when I was a pip squeak.
                And I remember Friday nights
                    when he'd turn on the TV.
              I don't know who killed Davey Moore
                     I sure hope it wasn't me.
My father was a middleweight,
and many years ago.
he fought the onion farmer from upstate
Carmen Basilio.
He lost a split decision
and he never boxed again;
while the little goomba took a belt away
from Ray Robinson.
                  I remember Friday nights
                    when he'd turn the TV on.
            I was watching the night Griffith proved
                    he weren't no maricón.
I remember Gillette safety blades
Carling Black Label beer—
a sizzling gray fireplace and
daddy's cauliflower ear.
I remember pretty Cassius Clay
stinging like a bee
when he was still a negro
before he became Ali.

My father was a middleweight—
he thought bigger guys were slow.
He told me Ali was more than great,
the best we'd ever know.

And I remember Friday nights
when he'd turn on the TV.
I don't know who killed Davey Moore
I sure hope it wasn't me.

My father was a middleweight,
the golden gloves he won.
He died when he was 48
and I was 21.

Sometimes I think he'd be surprised
at the softness of my hands
that never had to work too much
I hope he understands.

# THE PRESIDENT NEXT DOOR

We decided we weren't the sort of folks
who could thrive in the economically
homogeneous sunblasted suburbs
of far west Little Rock, Arkansas.

Not that there is anything wrong with it,
but everyone there has an SUV,
a jogging stroller with pneumatic tires,
and clips their grass to airbase specs.

So we started looking and finally found
a house that suited us
back in the old neighborhood.

It was owned by a Friend of Bill,
and it was in a cul de sac
and it was just below
the crest of a hill
(the best place, Frank Lloyd Wright always said)
and if you stood on the roof
or on the highest point of the backyard
you could see a browngray
patch of the Arkansas River.

We tore out walls, rewired the kitchen and discovered
beneath geological layers of carpet and teak parquet
some "amazing" hardwood floors.

And two doors down
in one of the expensive condominiums
lived the mother-in-law
of the then-current
President of the United States.

This was presented to us as a selling point.

It also explained
the ganglia of cables
the house inspector ripped
from the crawlspace
and held up in the sunlight
like a fisherman

brandishing his glinting, dying catch.
They were, we were told, communication lines
placed there by the Secret Service who "billeted"
the president's personal physician there
on the two or three
times a year
POTUS came back to Little Rock.

They—the Secret Service—
liked to put POTUS up
in his mother-in-law's condo
because it was an easier location
to secure than any of the downtown hotels.
And besides,
she was family.

The week after we (finally) moved in
we threw a party
to show off our new digs.

A few days before the party
we were visited
by a Secret Service agent named
Sculley.

He informed us there was a chance
—just a chance, mind you, nothing for certain—
that POTUS would be staying in the condo
over the weekend.

Was there anything they should know?

Being patriotic, we offered to cancel our party
but Sculley wouldn't have it.
There was only a chance
That POTUS would be here anyway because
he wanted to fly to Fayetteville
after his speech and see the Razorbacks play basketball.
Anyway, Sculley said,
we were not to worry, but
just in case, could I provide a guest list?

"If he's here," Sculley said,
"he might even walk up
to say hello
and spend a few minutes at the party—
he probably won't but he's done strange things
like that before.
Once he even ditched us.
He cut through your backyard
to I Street
where a friend picked him up
and they drove off
for a couple of hours."

"I probably shouldn't tell you this," he said

And so I typed out
a list of all the names
of all the people
we had invited to the party
and I told Agent Sculley
there were likely some names that I'd forgotten
and he said that was okay,
They would just call us
if someone who wasn't on their list showed up at the checkpoint.

The next day there was an awful-looking motorhome,
a dingy gray-green leviathan,
parked in front of our house
and lots of polite policemen
and darksuited agents
with coiled wires
running out their collars
to their ears.

On the night of our party
we had rain and forks of lightning
and so POTUS was grounded
and a roadblock was set
at the foot of the hill.

And all our guests
got frisked and bomb-sniffing dogs
set on their cars
while a man
with a mirror on a pole
checked for explosives
that might be strapped to undercarriages.

We only had one guest refuse
to run that gantlet.

(Griffin Smith.
An editor with libertarian leanings.
He refused  to subject himself to search
and so his wife didn't speak to him
all the way home.)

My friend Doug Thompson
approached me
to ask how I knew
his full name
because he never used it.

And it was on the list
the cops had at the bottom of the hill.

I told him I didn't know it
and that I'd only given them
the barest bit of information.

Later I would find out
they did background checks because
of the time when John Wayne Gacy
had his picture
snapped with Rosalynn Carter.

"They caught holy hell for that one,"
I was told much later
by a golf buddy,
who for a time had been detailed
to the Carter White House.

It wasn't really fair though,
because Mr. Gacy was a Democratic precinct captain
at the time and not any kind of suspect.

During the party
a number of our guests huddled together in our bedroom
to stare through the window that afforded
a good look at the front door of the condo
where POTUS was staying
as well as the presidential limo
and the decoy president limo
and the black SUVs
that choked up our little cul de sac
and required our guests
to hoof it
a block or so to reach the party.

That's why we still call our bedroom "the sniper's nest."

POTUS didn't show that night.

(In fact, in all the years he stayed there,
he never walked up to say hello
though he knew who we were
and always smiled and waved
when we saw him in the street.)

The next day
My wife Karen was in the backyard
and Sculley came up to her
and asked if all had gone well at the party
the night before.

She said it had and
then he asked her
if we had gotten to see POTUS
and she said, "Yes, from our bedroom window,
we have a clean—"

"Don't say 'shot,'"
he said.

These days in my neighborhood, one sees
bumper stickers reading:
"I miss Bill."

And I do too.
But not the motorhome.

# GASTONIA, N.C.

## (art song in D)

Irene Bell was 22
in 19 and 34
after the Crash, before she knew
the strivings of an Asheville whore.

She'd come from a good family.
Not good enough, apparently.
Her mother prayed the rosary.
Her father lost all the money.

There are times it all comes clear.
There are times it seems so simple.
A word went in her daddy's ear;
a bullet in her daddy's temple.

And the boy she married wandered off
to look for work in Tennessee.
He left her nothing but his name
and an inconvenient pregnancy.

Her baby's eyes were bright and black
fastened on some long horizon.
Where the Devil drives a Cadillac
—a V–16 dual cowl Phaeton.

The Minnesota man was sad.
Sadder than a stillborn pup.
Sad because his wife was mad.
Irene knew how to cheer him up.

But her own capacity for hope
was crushed out in the rooms she let
by frightened men with rabbit eyes
cutting at the bassinet.

The Devil's eyes are cobalt blue,
his kiss burns like a cigarette.
His touch is enough to make you do
things you know that you'll regret.

Her second son—Jack—never knew
a father or facsimile.
*À la recherche du temps perdu*:
A case for Catholic charity.

So now you ask me where I'm from?
Scotch-Irish, Welsh and grain whiskey,
tobacco spit and soldier's cum
along with some French and Cherokee.

# THE SENTINEL
### (three chords and the truth)

Shagged my ass to Vietnam
when I was but nineteen years old
as proxy for my Uncle Sam
doing only what I's told.

Burned some gook kid on patrol
and they kitted out a ribbon rack.
Hoochie coochie rock 'n' roll
I served my tour and then went back.

Then I gut stuck an officer
behind the whore house in Da Nang.
I didn't like the way he looked at her
but I loved the way my senses rang.

Dude had a rendezvous with Death
as do you and as do I.
But when I feel the bastard's breath
I'll spit right in the devil's eye.

I came home and my congressman
got me a job on state police.
Because I'm a great American
a brother who will keep the peace.

I give no fucks for the chief,
nor party boss nor president.
Nor for the families on relief—
I understand how I am bent.

So pray to the god that you have made,
ask him please your soul to keep.
Hell ain't got nothing I can't fade
I watch for monsters while you sleep.

# JESUS CLARK

Jesus would have been a carpenter,
had his parents had their way.
But their boy had his own big ideas,
and things he thought he had to say.
So he went off to Iowa
to pursue his MFA.

He wrote sonnets and short stories,
a few of which survive.
And worked on a bildungsroman
that recalls Slaughterhouse Five.
While he did all his teachers asked,
he couldn't make himself work harder.
So though he displayed some talent,
he never had a poet's ardor.

He had some doggerel published
in a little magazine.
But when some balding jerk
dismissed his work
Jesus quit the academic scene
for a tour of duty
in the Merchant Marine.

After Jesus mustered out,
he seemed to lose his way.
He wandered around the desert some,
he sold plasma in L.A.
He hung around the Sunset Strip
and worked on a screenplay
about a prophet in the porno biz
and his jihad on cliché.

Jesus worked various jobs
in the service industry.
He probably had a brief romance
with the (female) maitre d'
of a trendy little bistro
in Century City.

But the city of the angels
proved too amorphous for JC
so he hitchhiked up the coast
to Vancouver, B.C.
where he started writing book reviews
for an alternative weekly.

It was at the Barb his politics
took on a distinctly pinkish hue,
but few people read his pieces
and those who did already knew
that the times they were a'changing
and bills were comin' due.

So Jesus went and cut his hair
and got on the methadone.
Bought a dead man's suit from a thrift shop
and called his mother on the phone.
She cashed in her IRA
to fly the prodigal boy home.

Jesus signed up for night courses
and took a civil service test.
He worked evenings in his father's shop
and soon became obsessed
with earning his real estate license
and becoming the very best.

And he felt robustly blessed.

Now you see Jesus's face around
on billboards and bus benches.
Smiling down from on high,
twist-tied to chain link fences.
He's got the sort of face you trust.
a gaze they call beatific.
He might have washed out as a philosopher,
but as a salesman, he's terrific.

# BLACK ICE

Rain came early Christmas morning,
and we knew what that meant:
A glaze of smashed crystal
spread micron thin,
Tefloning the roads
and trapping us within
memories pitched
like the invisible fences
that hold in
growling Rockefeller dogs
when their wrought iron gate swings open.

My wife put on her yoga CD
of Jud Martindale's drumming
because she couldn't—
wouldn't—
chance it running on the streets
not even with our YakTrax
or the StablIcers
that came all the way from roadless Maine
and allow whoever has the chore
of walking up the bobsled run
to do so safely
and with confidence.

A few years before,
when we lived in the suburbs,
I stepped out of the garage
onto our driveway and
touched
my boot to the polished concrete.
and up I went
like some Chuck Jones coyote
suspended for an instant
like a curse
in the cold air.

I slipped again
two years ago
on Hill Road
on the sidewalk
on a patch I never noticed

until after  I was lying on my back.
And so
I lifted weights in the chilly sunroom
with the leaking windows
and the cracked concrete floor
while my breath made fog
while the drums thrummed and chanted
and Karen
flexed and supinated
around the investigative noses of our dogs.

We made coffee
and opened presents
and celebrated
—in the wry ironic way we have—
our circumscribed continent
of souls
apart from the world that troubles us;
a world full of asperity and spite and the selfishness of small hearts.

She asks me if I remember
the squirrel who
shorted out the transformer
and fell (dead before he hit the ground)
into our yard.

His eyes were Xed, I said
like Krazy Kat
in the old comics
after Ignatz Mouse (his/her beloved)
beaned him/her with a brick.

He never saw it coming.

We are the only ones who do
and we don't really.

We assume the road goes on
around the bend, over the hill
and that our feet will hold.
We assume we have a purchase on this rock,
that time will reveal to us some satisfying pattern,
that the universe will one day yield
to the confabulations of our vain imaginations.
Because it must.

An exploding transformer
is not a car bomb.
I know.

And the most dangerous ice
is the thinnest.
The kind you can't even see.

# Bad Brain

We were watching baseball on TV—
a playoff game,
Cleveland at Seattle.

In the seventh inning
Coal—our Lab, a mixed breed actually—
juddered and jackknifed.

Pissing and foaming,
a snap of black muscle—
when I pinned him,
his eyes were the color of old pennies and dumb hurt.

I did not recognize the seizure for what it was.
I thought he was choking
on a rawhide strip.

So for a moment
I held in my hand
your Swiss Army knife
—a cool balance of steel—
as I  tried to make myself
slice into his doggish throat.

I lacked the nerve
to perform the tracheotomy
I thought would save his life.
Instead I stood there
as you jammed your hand into his mouth
and pulled it back
empty
and bleeding.

He stopped kicking and twitching
and lay panting.
For a while
he didn't know us.
Then he did.

We cleaned him up
and bandaged your hand
and you called the emergency 24-hour vet
while I went and poured myself
a Big Gulp of Scotch
and sat down trembling and stinking
of sweat and fear.

Was that a pine floor?
In my memory, it is so dark.

2.

Sometimes I wake up feeling guilty
of some crime I can't remember.

It is after midnight
and you sleep on unaware
of the murderer beside you.
I am so scared, sweetheart,
I am so afraid
that what I was before I knew you
might track us down.

*Lustmord.*
A German word.
Lamplight on linoleum
in the student ghetto
north of L.S.U.
(Not Tiger Town,
with its suburban debutantes
and Sigma Chis.)

Walking by
I saw her face in the mirror
through the window.
She brushed her hair
in her slip.

3.

We are what we do
and also what we might have done
had we the nerve.

But this is crazy talk;
it is late and you are warm.
And my exile will be over
when I get up from my desk
and walk those few blind steps to our bed,
pausing just a moment
to touch Coal's fevered, sleeping head.

# FIRST BODY

I walked out and stood where the Cajun detectives smoked
on the gray lawn and
looked up at stars piercing
a night clear, cruel and cold
as freezered vodka.

She's young, I said.
"That's so," said Elton,
"her mama young and so's her granny too.
Her sister who dun dun her, younger even than she.
Why you tink they keep they house so warm?"

(Murder houses always have that
dry warm feeling
and oily light
that makes the bodies
look like waxworks.)

Inside: The child carcass,
a rusted scissors in its heart.
Blond-eyed Jesus on the wall.

I didn't say she was my first
and they maybe didn't know
and they surely didn't care.
And they didn't make the jokes
that we reporters did
to indicate that we had seen it all and nothing
could shock us.

Instead they took the statements
of the young mother and young grandmother.
I took out my notebook
and tried to write a story like a poem.

# INCIDENT AT THE LITTLE UNION BAPTIST CHURCH
## Shreveport, September 22, 1963

The white man on the white horse
cantered through the flung-wide church door,
from out of the riotous sun
spilling across the pine plank floor,
and up the center aisle, his gun
flashing like a plastic chrome toy.

(It feels to me like a movie
I watched when I was still a boy.
And even now, remembering,
some ghost camera cuts and slides.
There is no set positioning—
the point of view is omniscient.)

The white man on the white horse
reeled and very smartly went
right up to Reverend Harry Blake
and smote him with his pistol butt.
I witnessed this; make no mistake—
cowering in the children's pew.

Now that I've stood in Sainte-Chapelle
I know our church was poor. It's true
I felt ashamed and criminal.
(And, damn me, I guess I still do).
My heart flew to the strong white man
who beat the meek black preacher down.

There were bombs in Birmingham
and talk of marches going round.
Blake had reached out to Doctor King—
but this was Shreveport, D'Artois's town.
And he would have no such a thing;
no Commie nigra stirring shit.

There wasn't: King, he never came.
The lawmen kept a lid on it.
D'Artois wore a white felt hat
when the mayor handed him a plaque.
I never thought it funny that
things were different for black.

# BILLY BOB THORNTON

Billy Bob Thornton
called me up
just to say
that he liked it when I interviewed him because
I never not even once
asked him if he was
a vampire.

I said I appreciated his noticing
and we talked about
Arkansas,
and how there were guys
working in the Peavey plant
who could play guitar
every bit
as good as
Jimi Hendrix.

And how some of them
manage to be happy
despite the fact
they are not
immortal.

# THANKSGIVING

### (for d.l.)

We went into the alkaline hills
childless and arrogant
to meet your friends
with our chianti and tupperware
in running shoes and silk sweaters
—jeans against jumping cactus,
canvas jackets for the shadows' chill.

Your invitation surprised me.
A fat envelope announcing
"You may already be a winner."
I knew your reputation, Red:
"The editor's ex-mistress"
according to the office gossip.

It was my first month working there.
I was the youngest in the newsroom.
And I was the most alone.
It was never what they might have thought.
Or what I wanted: You were kind.

I don't much remember the others—
friends of yours, a married couple,
the goateed man an artist of some sort.
He talked to me of basketball
of Barkley and Thunder Dan
as our campfire and the darkness

conspired with the carbohydrates
the wine and the way you cut your eyes
(checking on my conversation )
to fix me in the amber glow
of that parody of family.
That is how I still remember you.

We were never lovers. You know that.
We just ran together for a while.
And if you ever thought I loved you—
well, I did but not so much as
I feared some fragile crazy drama
softly blowing on my neck.

I was a coward, sure—a wormboy.
Maybe I was only acting.
I can't swear that I was honest
with you always and forever.
I can't swear I never cursed you
or that you ever felt a thing.

I just remember that Thanksgiving,
the way you laughed and flipped your hair.
How we talked of Raymond Chandler
and the mating rites of Mormons.
I told you all about the South
and the churches I had been in.

I was out there for fourteen months.
A tour of duty in the badlands.
We lost touch after I moved on.
I heard it through the grapevine
you were excommunicated.
I didn't realize that mattered—
you'd joked about their underwear.

Someone tracked me down in Arkansas
because they thought I ought to know
your disease had overtaken you.
You rented a cabin by the sea
where you thinned your blood with vodka
and cut your way out with a razor.

I do not presume I could have saved you.
I only glimpsed the vaulting mania—
I never rocked you in the creeping darkness.
I protected myself at all times
and broke clean when the whistle screamed.
I no doubt saved myself a few regrets.

My luck has held; I've given up old grievances.
I've forgotten my enemies' names,
and learned to do the best I can
with this odd and wounded world
that, like me, cannot imagine its own dying.

# ARKANSAWYERS

(electric blues in E)

I hear what they say about us
in the goddamn *New York Times*.
They say we're backward and we're ignorant.
I can read between the lines
when the *Wall Street Journal*
references "Arkansas mores."
Louis Jordan came from Brinkley,
he *ne parle pas Francais*.

We're the people they fly over
when they move from coast to coast.
They think of us as specimens,
as Compsons and as Snopes.
Think everything good down here
is some kind of accident.
Well, you mightn't like Bill Clinton, sir,
but he's still your president.

Some people call you cracker
Some people call you poor white trash.
Some people call you redneck.
Some call you country ass.
They can call you anything they want,
they can't make you go away.
John Cash weren't from New York City,
he didn't grow up in L.A..

I ain't sayin' that we're better stuff
or that we always do the best we can.
I'm just sayin' that I've had enough
of being talked down to by some man
who thinks Andrea Mitchell
knows what folks here can understand.

They can call us Miller Williams,
They can call us Bill Fulbright
They can call us Maya Angelou—
"Arkansawyer" sounds all right.

# FLOOD DOGS

We were watching
the Katrina coverage
of the relentless waters
with the bloated bodies bobbing
like toys
in the bloodbrown bog
and the diapered children
on the rooftops
waving.

It was terrible, we agreed,
and sad to think
of the ruin of the city
and the plight—the *plight*—
of the poor.
But what made us cry
was the woman
who couldn't take her dog
in the rescue boat.

She had to choose,
the police said.
They could shoot it
or cut its throat. Either way
she wouldn't have to watch.

*Dogs make us better,* my wife said
and I agreed.
*We couldn't leave ours.*

And I think
Hitler fed his shepherd cyanide.
Because he loved her.

I know there is something wrong with me
and that I won't get into Heaven.
But I have considered it
and I am quite sure
I do not love you, manunkind.
You unnatural beast
slinking with your antiseptic mercies,

your cruel science
and *savoir faire.*
Maybe I now stand
with the Indian
—I mean, Native American
(or, as we might say in supersecret,
"woo woo"), as opposed to
("red dot") Asian Indian—
gentleman in the movie
who said we shouldn't worry
because one day
after we've killed off
one another
with our politics and religion
the Earth will be able to relax
and breathe
and the rivers will come back
and forests will grow
and life will
once again
tingle
nastily
in the grass.

# 1993

I am afraid that you might see
all these petty appetites
that gnaw away at decency,
that got me through the desert nights.

I know a wilderness within,
a no man's land, a dry empire
where a jackal with a rictus grin
pulls at the heart tangled in wire.

I toss upon a sea of black,
lidded by a metal sky.
There are no stars by which to track,
no progress to identify.

And with no ballast to my soul,
no conviction to hold me right,
I might pitch from side to side,
I might capsize in the night.

Yet if my fever breaks with you,
slippery, yet adhered to me.
I might say things that might be true.
I might not feel so damn lonely.

# CLOSEST FRIEND

## (acoustic version)

Sometimes I wake to watch you sleep,
moonlight eddied in your hair.
If I prayed I'd ask the gods to keep
you safe and to repair
all the damage I have done,
all I may ever do,
and never let me wake up
in a world without you.

I know how good my luck has been
and how provisional it felt—
when I was in the badlands
with Teddy Roosevelt.
Then there were times I wasn't sure
I could ever make it clear.
When I didn't think I wanted to,
when I was sleeping with the fear.

Somehow you came and got me
took me in and set me straight,
brought me to your little house
where I could recuperate.
You helped me unpack my heart,
and throw the bitterness away.
You negotiated with my past,
and then you let me stay.

Sometimes I fear there's something wrong with me
I cannot eradicate.
Some stupid male inconstancy
that makes me hesitate.
Some blind white whale who now and then
rolls in the waters of my core.
But I swear I'm telling you the truth
I don't do that anymore.

And I've heard it said all writing
is a war upon cliché.
But earnest words are all I have,
there's nothing I can say,
except I know the smooth curve of your hip
like I know my very breath.
I know you are my closest friend
and I will love you unto death.

# THE BOY IN THE BOOKSTORE

I was working as a cop reporter,
not fully resigned to the adult world
and all its incumbencies and obligations
when a girl I knew a little
was strangled in her apartment
off Highland Avenue
near Centenary College.

It was a room over a garage
with student furniture
and paperbacks
and silk scarves draped
poetically
over lampshades
and incense holders with black stained sockets.

The detective said
when the neighbor found her
the record player was still spinning
its needle bumping
at the end of — guess what? —
Eddy Grant's *Killer on the Rampage*.

This was great stuff for my story.
What we call
a "significant detail."

She worked in the bookstore
in the Pierre Saint Vincent Mall.
I saw her there sometimes
a glasses-wearing girl,
who chewed on pencils,
and tucked her light hair behind her ears,
and smiled at the backs of customers
browsing in the literature section.

Later I would go
and see the boy
who the cops had (off the record)
identified as a suspect.
He was a manager there
and a graduate student,
a nervous knotty boy
with thin ginger hair
that flared and fizzed
like a sparkler
dropped by a freckled ten-year-old girl
in the dry dust
of a Missouri dirt road
on a Fourth of July night.

I saw him reading Vico's Scienza Nuova
behind the counter
his lip trembling.

I knew that it was him.
And he was the same as me.
I never said three words to him.
We just nodded
as he counted out my change.

It's always the boyfriend,
the detectives told me.
*It's always who you think it is.*
And, you know,
some of them
aren't so evil really,
it's just the moment,
the really bad moment,
that we all have to get through,
that they can't get through.

When the time comes to prove you are a man
you have to walk away from it
if you can.

Women will kill
but only for a reason,
not for a look
or the lack of one.
Or because they thought
they were
or could be
someone different.

Male fragility is dangerous
and difficult to track
sometimes.
Unless the killer is standing there,
confessing,
crying,
complaining,
about how the body done him wrong,
we hardly ever can make a case.

Once they get themselves
away,
and composed,
they can see
how it truly was.
And that
they only did
what they were made to.

The boy in the bookstore
was never arrested
or publicly identified,
and after a while he moved away
and even I stopped thinking
about the case.

Except
sometimes
when I drove by the apartment
and I wondered who
had rented it
and if she knew
what had happened there
and if
there was a ghost
sitting on the edge of the bed
watching
as she tied ribbons
in her hair
and misted perfume
in the air
to dew upon
her yet unblemished breasts.

# THE MONEYLOOKER

"Everyone needs money. That's why they call it money."
—David Mamet via Danny DeVito in *Heist*

I look for change in the street.
It is a bad habit, I know.
But I like to walk
and I like to find money
and often I do.

It's not just that I am lucky,
I see things that other people don't.

Which makes me an artist.
And thereby entitled to
whatever dribbled crumbs I can snatch;
the dimes and the nickels
(I don't stoop for pennies)
and the occasional scrap of paper
you regular folks probably thought was just a
Jack Chick
bait and switch tract.

("Damn, it's not a dollar. Just the *Road to Salvation*.)

Once I found a five hundred cruzerio note
on the beach
by the Hotel Intercontinental
in Rio de Janeiro.
It sounds like a lot
(and it was to me at the time, for I was nearly broke)
but it was really only about twenty-five dollars American.

And there was the time in New York's
Little Italy
on New Year's Eve
when Brian's wife Barbara
found a twenty-dollar bill in the gutter.
It was right after we saw
the ratasbigasapuppy
scuttle by—
not like he was in a hurry—
and you said
he probably left it as a tip for
the boys who hauled the garbage out
and piled it in the dumpster.

Well, I never told you
but I saw it first.

And I only let her find it
because I wanted her
to know the thrill
of buying our tiramisu.

Brian is a doctor, sure,
I get that but
it's really not about the money —
if the money amounted to anything
I'd give it all away to charity
or fund a hospital.

Money is just the paper
I wave around to convince the world
of my mental health.
I am an entrepreneur
like Trump and J.P. Morgan
and
all the other great men.

I just prefer to work
on a more human
scale.

# SHERPA SONG
## (straight four-four rock 'n' roll)

*(For our dog Sherpa, a girl of unknown provenance whom we adopted on a whim after meeting her in PetSmart while she was being fostered by a sweet teen-ager named Kelly who called her "White Dog," and who after more a decade still won't let me approach her or scratch her ears without running away. Even so, we thought she deserved a backstory to go along with her fictive personality.)*

*One, two, three, four . . .*

She was a trailer park Lhasa from Bryant.
He was the poodle from the top of the hill.
One night when she was feeling compliant
he left his yard in pursuit of a thrill.

They had a late night assignation
and she hasn't seen his tail since.
Though nightly he bays his frustration
from within an Invisible Fence.

When puppies spilled forth like cheap candy
from a piñata burst by a brat,
some resembled their father, the dandy,
others looked more unlovely than that.

None of them were show dogs in waiting,
some were lucky, some loved and some were not.
Then a painted old hag stuck some rocks in a bag
and threatened to drown the whole lot.

It was in the sad den of dysfunction,
our Sherpa's story begins.
Though she was just a pup, she said, "Please to shut up.
That's why you don't have any friends."

This so shocked the mobile home hussy,
that she left the poor doggies alone.
Mama Lhasa got wise, and said, "Listen, you guys,
I think you'd be better off gone."

They scattered all over the county
like a pandemic of avian flu.
When Sherpa gave it a try, she found out she could fly,
weekdays from eleven 'til two.
She finally crash-landed in Benton,
where she discovered she needed some cash,
to buy hair barrettes and Kool cigarettes.
So she took a job slinging bacon and hash.

You might not think much of this story
about a little white mop of a cur,
it's not hard to see she got no pedigree
but no dog is loved more than her.

# THE LOVE SONG OF HENRY LEE LUCAS

Detective captain sir.
Killing one's mother
is not so hard as burning a bridge
or brushing over one's tracks with a frond.
It is a way of releasing,
of uncoupling one's self
from history.

She was my first challenge,
a one-legged whore
who wanted no more
than a bottle and money
to buy her
snuff.

# BROTHER BOB

(Blues in E)


Brother Bob was bad to drink;
Mother's baby and her pride.
She wrote him lots of checks, I think,
and seeded dreams of regicide.

Our father was a stalwart cuss,
red-assed, tall and strong and spare.
He'd look Jesus in the eye
and tell the puss to cut his hair.

I was the oldest—semi-queer,
a bookish boy, a bit effete.
Pop sometimes swore when I could hear
he must have strained me through a sheet.

And Jeff, the middle boy, worked hard
to be his father's favorite son.
But Jeff was halfway a retard;
which didn't impress Daddy none.

Pop slapped us some but not too much;
he never closed his fist on me.
Jeff may have known a rougher touch
but Mom made him let Bobby be.

Still Robert was the rowdy one;
bad to drug, he burglarized
a coach's car after they'd won
some stupid fuckin' football prize.

Kicked out of school, Bob moved in
with Jeanette from the waffle shop,
who hooked a little on the side
and whose ex-husband was a cop.

What happened in that rented room
I couldn't say, I wasn't there.
Dad's blood was splattered on the wall—
They couldn't find him anywhere.

And Bobby and Jeanette were gone
Presumed absconded — fugitive.
I heard Mother whispering on the phone;
I haven't any evidence to give.

I haven't evidence to give
not that I'd give it if I could:
Some people don't deserve to live.
Sometimes Evil does some good.

# URBAN SHOCKER

### (a banjo song)

My name is Urban Shocker.
I played baseball for a spell.
If people don't remember me
I guess it's just as well.

I came down from Ohio,
not to work the mills or farm,
I squatted down behind the plate,
but the scouts preferred my arm.
So I worked up a dropsy pitch,
a roundhouse and a hook,
a crooked finger change-up—
I kept me a hitters' book.

Miller Huggins bought my contract,
then sold me to the Browns.
I always liked St. Louis,
one of your better baseball towns.
But even with George Sisler,
we never got it done.
Though I won me twenty-seven games
In 19 and 21.

I always vexed the Yankees,
that murderous crew of lore,
so they traded for me
In 19 and 24.

Truth be told I felt it then,
wet and heavy in my chest.
We slumped a bit in '25
and I failed to impress.

But I came back in 1926,
there was something in the air.
To keep down my pneumonia
I slept in my rocking chair.
We took home the pennant but
the Cards beat us fair and square.

No, if people don't remember me
I don't guess that's a crime.
But in 1927,
we were the greatest of all time.

# Ray Chapman, Killed by Pitch, August 16, 1920

### For Mike Coolbaugh

I had it in my mind to bunt
but something in the crowd distracted me—
a wrinkle in the hazel sea.

High and tight, underhanded heat
I never saw.
The sound—
a whitesick pop.
The ground.
Carl Mays looking down.
A bruised baseball rolling to the second baseman's feet.

I got up and took my base,
a warm rivulet,
etching acid,
on my face.

# THE APOSTATE

My father was a ballplayer;
my earliest memories of him:
a fine baseline silt
and a catcher named Bucky
who, on a backfouled ball,
would spin and throw his mask
so fiercely
it would ring in the chain link backstop.

("Never loop your fingers
through the fence," I was advised,
"A ball could bust them.")

My father was the shortstop—
a little hotdog.
He would scoop up grounders
and hold them for what seemed
more than a full second
looking down into his Rawlings glove
like a far-sighted man reading a menu
as though each baseball held for him
some coded message.

Then he would set himself and with
a darling little hop
whip the ball through the bright air
into the first baseman's patient
yawning mitt.

The umpire would signal
with the smallest of gestures
as if to minimize
the runner's shame
of being out.

2.

When I was a high school senior
my father took me to dinner
with a Red Sox scout he knew
from the old days.

I was skinny then and fast enough
and could hit.
(I loved to hit.)

I burned to sign my name
on some piece of paper
to mortgage my youth
for the slimmest chance of putting off
being grown-up
and playing in the grass and dirt
and being called a "scrapper."

I didn't dare to dream of glory
or bonus money
but I thought I could play a little
and that maybe
I might have earned the good opinion
of the Red Sox scout
who'd seen me go three-for-four
with a double and make a diving stop
to save a run.

My father, younger then than I am now,
did not see it the same way.
He had never made the majors
though he knew lesser men who had.
He was of the opinion
that I ought to go to school and read
Robert Graves and Tennyson's
"The Charge of the Light Brigade."

*All in the valley of Death,*
*Rode the six hundred.*

I was bigger than he was
but not big really
and if we'd raced that night
in our church shoes
down Youree Drive
he would have beaten me.

At my father's behest, the scout showed me his report:
the cool black facts of appraisal.
I was no good,
not really—
just a kid
quick hands, slow feet
an arm as dead
as the taxman's dreams of heaven.

All in all I think I took the saneness pretty well.
In the Steak and Lobster
while the men sipped bourbon
I was allowed
a glass of bitter beer.

3.

I still tell that story sometimes
over wine
because I believe it makes me seem more interesting
to have had the kind of past
in which I'd had dinner with a scout.

My father is twenty years dead this day
and I swear I bear him no rancor.
I swear I understand why he thought
he was only doing what
needed to be done.
I never held that night against him.

My wife does not agree with me;
She thinks—she senses—
that it was unnecessary cruelty,
some vain male stupid gesture
from a father who would not be surpassed.

I say it was only baseball,
a church to which I once belonged
before I lost my faith.

# Shook

My wife doesn't like me to go on about
the old days. And she's right.
There's nothing so pathetic as a grown man
telling you about the night
he went for fifty-two points
against the Wampus Cats.

Their Alaskan Indian
six foot six, if he was an inch,
jumped up, cracked his head on the backboard;
but refused to come out of the game.
He played on, blood drizzling down his face.
And that's what everyone remembers.

Still, it was my night of attenuated grace
when my feet were quick and my hands were sure
and every time I touched the ball
I shot it high and soft and pure.
And even Sammy Joyner looked to me
and nodded in his doleful way.

Just boys together
action-painting,
squeaking sneakers,
leaping, sweating, anticipating
the day we'd sit
on barstools waiting
for our wives to ground us with that look.

She shakes her head and I get shook.

# THE PRY BAR

"It was cathartic," you say now
when you tell our demolition story to guests
who wonder at the openness
of our rooms and how they got that way.
We took a sledge, smashed the iron tub
to shards, ripped down walls and
in the evenings sat on plastic tarp
and wept for other lives foreclosed.

And though I did not know myself
I would tell you (I would promise you)
we were all right and would be still
after writing the carpenter's check
and paying for the cabinets
custom-ordered for our kitchen.
"Numbers are just numbers," I decreed,
in my best basso big boy voice.

Then one day I stuck our ripping tool
—the pry bar—in the bathroom wall.
It caught; I strained and pulled it out
reaping a whirlwind of drywall smut.
When the cloud cleared, the pry bar was
stuck deep in my side, beneath my ribs.
"Forthwith there came out blood and water,"
I remember thinking to myself.

You cleaned the gash with peroxide.
It never stung. We bandaged it
and when it healed it left on my skin
a raised filament, a white seam.
That, months later, was remarked upon
by Doctor Stephen Tilley
who asked me how this tidy scar came to be.
I shared the tale. He doubted me.

It didn't happen like that, he said:
It must have been in Mexico
when you stepped in with common sense
to referee a dispute between
two criminal biker chieftains.
They shook hands in the cantina,

your work was done, but on the sidewalk
a prospect looking to make his bones
shivved you between the ribs.

Your forgiveness didn't save him.
They buried his parts in the alkaline
wasteland of del Notre de Sonora and
when they dropped you across the border
at the American hospital, they warned you:
"Never speak of this, *mi amigo*,
tell them you did it remodeling."

And so I tell the pry bar story.

Now, on the occasions I touch the scar
and am forced back unwittingly,
it is Tilley's version that prevails
over the dull dumb domestic facts
of the demolition accident.
I believe it—
for there were times when I was younger,
more afraid, and full of hunger.

Before you, there was the Christmas in Chicago
when the kid with the screwdriver
and the broken teeth and broken pride
tried to take my money
outside of married student housing
at the U. of C.: It was his blood,
not mine, on the sidewalk,
embeamed by police flashlights,
leading South down Cottage Grove.
I had hurt him.

And she—the one before you—was frightened
by my fury and desperation
by my unregulated eyes.
By the way I kept on hitting him
after I caught him in the doorway.
I went to a hotel that night
and rolled over in my mind,
hard and unproveable theories about myself.

She and I were having our troubles then.
It might have been I wanted to die
defending her; just to show
I wasn't like the others that
she sometimes spoke to me about
the wormboys and the brutish men
 like the one who held the pistol
(unloaded, she believed and hoped)
to his own head as she fellated him.

What was it *she* had wanted?
Something unvoiceable and cruel?
Did she want to cry for me struck down
and bleeding, my life stuff leaching out,
her poor martyred blondboy husband
killed and gone away forever?
It was my fault, my striving,
my persistent male unsated need.
I could have given him the money.
Numbers are just numbers, after all.

And our scars are just evidence of old hurts,
impotent as bills long paid
languishing in old file boxes,
good for nothing but reminding us
of times we thought we had it rough.
Sometimes beneath my shirt I find it,
the spot where the pry bar caught me.
I rub it for luck; now I know:
It was just a scratch.

I see now I lived for you.
Somehow I found the leverage
to make the discontentment give,
to snap it into dust and powder.
I am glad for the murder
of the man I might have been.
The explosion
that hurtled me into your arms.
That put the pry bar in my hand.

# CLARK KENT SHOOTS BASKETS
## IN THE SMALLVILLE HIGH GYM

I miss enough; no one suspects
that these Buddy Holly glasses
disguise a freak. Lonely as God
I pump up threes. Every third one
I bang off the front of the rim.

"Elevate, Clark!" My coaches hiss,
prescribing more jump squats,
plyometrics and toe raises.
I nod, and will myself to sweat,
an alkaline tear trickling.

I am not the star; I play D
and break our opponents' presses.
I am the two-handed chest passer;
I box out and dive for loose balls.
No one notices my knees won't scrape.

Or that I never take a charge.
I cannot hurt them, though I know
the way it ends in ash and flame.
So I will bounce this basketball.
So I will play this fucking game.

What scares me more than kryptonite
is rumored immortality.
The thought of an eternal soul,
is cold anathema to me.

And so I shoot and miss and shoot
and only raise myself so high
for they are all I have to love
and all of them are going to die.

As will their world and universe.
And all their art and suffering
recorded in my super mind
will not amount to anything.

# ATOMS SPINNING

## (an inchoate rock opera)

If you met Peter in the street
you would not rush to greet him . . .

Just another man with thinning hair
and eyes that strain for color.
They could be gray, they might compare
with dun, or something duller.

Yet even so he's adequate
to most tasks most men must do
He lost love and felt well rid of it;
he's brokered comfort too.
In short he's lived a common life,
his libido wanes and waxes.
He's complied with all the petty laws
he's paid Caesarean taxes.

> "A doctor warms some stainless steel
> against poor Peter's skin.
> Hear his noises, low and soft,
> hear the scratching of his pen.
> His news is neither gay nor grim
> from our physician's point of view.
> (Are you glad to not be him?
> He'd rather not be you.)"

Some tumor hums behind his eye.
Peter knows that he must die.

He makes his way through shiny stillborn streets,
the white territories of his deathbed sheets
too much for his unwilling flesh to face
unbraced by alcohol and smoke.
He walks into a bar
and makes a joke.

Now he shrugs out of his coat
and hangs it like a traitor.
Slips a finger between knot and throat
and signals for the waiter.

"Bring a whiskey for the dying man;
and one for his long-dead father.
Here's a credit card that ought to scan,
and a dollar for your bother."
Hip-deep 'round Peter swim the ghosts
shark-silent, pale and nuzzling.
He bends his face up to the God
whose ways he finds so puzzling.
"You've rigged up Your universe,
so there's no point in resisting.
I'd ask You to leave me alone,
if I thought that You were listening."

(God doesn't notice Peter's prayer
or chooses to ignore him.
with a million kids to starve down there.
jerks like Peter bore Him.)

Peter raises up his cup
and tosses back his father's drink.
Goes to the men's room to throw up,
to toilet-sit and think.

2.

A clamor in a crowded car,
a skate punk with a backpack
a blonde girl with a big guitar
a flash, a crash, the shriekback . . .

And lucky Peter standing yet
amid the moans and crying.
The dead man lights a cigarette
and strolls among the dying.

When the first responders came
with their sirens and suspicions.
A policeman takes down Peter's name
then he's released—with conditions.

A light is shone in Peter's face
by an eager EMT.
Who says "God grants drunks especial grace.
You look OK to me."

Peter smiles a stupid smile,
brushes past a microphone,
stops to watch the fire a while
before starting out alone.

But spitting flecks of blood and foam
and stinking of disaster,
a black dog follows Peter home:
Sorrow cruising for a master.

3.

Peter fumbles at his door,
An hour after daylight.
Smelling of the night before;
of smoke and blood and cordite.

A gob of mercury in his head
lolls against the eggshell skull.
To the soft maw of an unmade bed,
he limps, dead-dicked and miserable.

He sleeps a medicated sleep
no dreams can penetrate.
He wakes within a stonewalled keep
and doesn't feel so great.

Sorrow licks his master's hand
as Peter sacks his closet
for a colored shirt to numb the hurt
and minimize his losses.

4.

Peter washed up in the vestibule,
with a thought of diving in
and polluting their most holy pool
with his turd of stinking sin.

Peter screaming in the church,
muffled by compassion.
As Jesus smiles down from his perch
upon the mortal passion.

Peter in the padre's face
sputtering and crying
against a pane of twice-glazed grace
and pity for the dying.

Peter slipping the priest's arm,
lurching from sanctuary,
setting off a car alarm
when he bounces off a Camry.

Wheeling in the parking lot,
floating like a feather,
hopeless as an astronaut
severed from his tether.

A jet of vomit on the ground
and sunlight lacerating.

Now Peter in a bright nightgown
in hospital, hallucinating:

Is this his doctor wandering in
to confirm the diagnosis?
He sweetly chucks at Peter's chin,
with a fistful of black roses.

> "I won't say 'I told you so',
> or any of that bullshit
> we all know that we gotta go
> but none of us believe it.
>
> But now you're hard against it, boy,
> the magic's due to expire
> and maybe you'll know sublime joy
> or be consumed by fire.
>
> I'm betting it will simply be
> a black forever yawning
> not even that; just vacancy,
> perpetual undawning.
>
> If that's the worst, you've not to fear
> for you're less real than this vision.
> We're riding on a phantom sphere
> there's no paradise—or prison.

There's only now. And now. And now —
worlds remade in an eye blink.
We do our best, and fail somehow
but it's not as bad as we think.

That's my dimestore philosophy;
sometimes I myself believe it.
Your bill's been figured. Nothing's free.
That's where we have to leave it."

So now Peter dies at last,
his bed a sparkling artic.
Devils mutter a gray mass.
hearts leaping in catharsis.

Do somewhere aggrieved angels sing?
Somewhere does someone listen?
Did Peter ever feel a thing
beyond some vague ambition

to be more than a slump of meat,
unblessed and just beginning
to be tickled by the divine heat
of atoms furiously spinning?

Your answer is as good as mine:
Thou shalt have no God above Him.
I made Peter up myself.
It's up to me to love him.

# September Morning NYC

"Two went down while holding hands
we never knew their names."
—Dan Bern, "NYC 9/11"


Concussed,
peeled alive,
born again in ripping wind and smoke
the howl, the oil, the cooking heat,
memory wiped,
history molted away and
a wheeling world beneath
his wing-tipped feet

Nameless, he watches
others drop like ancient tears
into a sea of newsreel gray.
How he knew
he could not fly
he really couldn't say.

(the curious lures of oblivion beckon
at thirty-two feet per second per second)

Amnesia's a blessing,
a sweet parting gift—
grief-shot he steps into the void
of horror film uplift.

# THE COPY EDITOR
## (12-string jingle for Woody Guthrie)

It's not quite correct to say I come from money—
we were upper lower middle class maybe.
Even so we had high expectations,
I always thought there'd be a place for me.

Now I'm sitting by the river in the Battery
with a quarter in my old Burberry coat.
Basking in God's grace, the sunshine on my face,
thinking about scratching out a note.

Like everybody else I went to college,
and them liberal arts, they seemed to serve me well.
I read a little Kafka and Jack London;
now I got this watch I really need to sell.

It's a Cartier Tank Normale 1917.
My grandfather brought it back from France.
After he fought in the war, that was gonna end all wars.
When he died it was my inheritance.

Yes sir, I understand your business model.
It ain't worth more than somebody's gonna pay.
But I'm worried they might mug me down on Avenue C
and I don't have no appointments anyway.

Forty years ago I was a hot shot.
I freelanced all over the Midwest.
I was doing fine, but then the *New York Times*
Offered me a spot on their copy desk.

Always thought there'd be time to write my novel.
Always grateful for the sinecure.
But though I liked the prestige and the paycheck,
there was part of me that always wanted more.

And so when they came and made their offer,
I took the buyout back in '93.
And I rented an apartment in the 8th arrondisement
*Je ne sais pas ce qui m'a pris.*

I spent the Clinton years holed up in Paris,
publishing the occasional essay.
And after 911, to go to Syria,
I cashed out my 401k.

Maybe I never had any real talent,
just a surfeit of self-esteem.
I've considered suicide, the Bowery gentrified,
seen the murder of the American dream.

# Idi Amin in Brazil

It took us most of the day
to climb Morro Dois Irmaos:
It was me and Steven Cherry,
and Cheri Gumm who was related
not-too-distantly to Judy Garland
(and had Joots' pleading smile)
and a ginger Brazilian
with a German name like Kaspar
who had been on Everest,
just a cook but even so
he was our leader, feeding out the lines
and wedging his nut tough body
into the rocky shallow hollows
that appeared like cheap contrivance
in a dull pulp mystery novel
whenever he required them.

I was not yet nineteen
but already I had sloughed off
most of my aspirations.
(They had moved me off of shortstop,
my arm wasn't strong enough.)

I reached up for a handhold,
one knuckle deep into a crevice,
and I strained and bucked and sweated,
with no technique to speak of,
yet I could pull myself higher,
if I looked only skyward
into the cool blue bitch of heaven.

I was twenty feet above Kaspar
(my anchor, giving safety)
when my tricep tore and I slipped,
scraping against the mountain,
tugged by gravity and hubris
into cold shock thoughtlessness
interrupted by the tautsnap
recoil of the climbing rope.

Kaspar held my shame dangling.
He said something easy, quiet,
and I put my hands on the rope
and climbed back up Batman-style.

I was wearing canvas Nikes,
early ones, designed for tennis,
not heavy boots like Kaspar's,
that could "kick holes in the mountain,"
and by the time I made the summit
their soft tread was nearly bald
and they smelled of burnt rubber.

There was a road down the mountain
that wound past gated estates
and skirted a favela
with kids beautiful and lithe—
gold fashion magazine urchins,
who stole ketchup from beachside cafes—
who hooted and laughed and hated
the American boys and girl
with their ropes and knifeblade pitons.

What I thought was a mosquito
turned out to be a wad of gum
chewed and rolled in crushed glass dust
shot (Kaspar said) from a blow gun.
It only stung a little bit
when it hit me in the neck.

When we got back to Kaspar's car
the radio was saying that
Idi Amin had been shot dead
on the streets of Kampala.

This was the recurrent rumor,
common as Sinatra music,
in the summer of '77
in Rio de Janeiro.

Brazil was obsessed with Amin.

The year before, in February,
Pelé had gone to Africa
to promote youth football (soccer).
They hadn't planned a Uganda stop
but the schedule opened up
so they flew into Entebbe,
then went on to the capitol.

Pelé was a New York Cosmo,
sponsored by Pepsi-Cola
but it was a Santos jersey
(the playmaker's No. 10)
he gave his Excellency,
the field marshall al hadji,
and President for Life Amin.

Uganda had some good soccer
and the school teams made Pelé smile
and applaud for their crisp crosses.
"Uganda is on the right track."
he told the hovering reporters,
"We must encourage young players,
they are the future of futbol."

In Nakivubo stadium
they arranged a game between
topflight yet oddly plodding sides:
Coffee and Uganda Prisons.
Pelé's limo left at half-time,
embarrassing Idi Amin.

The crowd jeered the government box,
the game crept to a goalless draw
and Amin swore voodoo vengeance
on Dico, and the Canarinho, and
Antônio Carlos Jobim.

So it was just wishfulness
on the part of Cariocas
that had the bad man slaughtered,
dragged through the streets and strung up
(like they did to Mussolini
in Giulino di Mezzegra).

Amin lived to be an old man,
an exile in the Novotel,
on Palestine Road in Jeddah,
protected by a Saudi prince.

He never understood his evil.

Now Pelé is an astronaut,
or a cartoon magician.
And I do not know what happened
to Cheri or to Kaspar though
I think Steve was a math teacher
in Southern California.
He might be near retirement now.

I flew over the rain forest
and then over the equator,
with cotton twisted on my wrist
and a figa
round my neck
for luck and protection.

There's a Botafogo jersey
that they gave me when I went home,
packed up somewhere in a closet
in my mother's house in Georgia
unless she gave it to her church
to send to kids in Africa,
who receive with calcium smiles
charity and genocide
or whatever is on offer.

# SHE

He moved and moaned; she stroked his back
and gazed up through the ceiling at the stars.
A wifely chore, a lovestruck whore,
another milk-run mission.
She makes her La Giaconda smile,
at his lack of inhibition.

She married him because she could
and no one else was bound to.
She loved him, for he was good,
and because he'd be around to
do the things that husbands should
and keep her from being ground down to
a nub of pretty girly nerve.

She let him think that he was wise—
she let him think he awed her—
that she thought he must be comprised
of *Übermensch*
and God the Father.

Some might say she's unfulfilled
or that she's somehow been unkind.
While he might believe he's thrilled,
flesh is weaker than the mind.
But if she took a second thought,
or a moment's hesitation,
it never once showed on her face
or upset her concentration.

For love's a practice; not a grace
bestowed on a lucky few.
It's wicked not to seek it out;
it's the least that you should do.

# A Card From the Mick

When my father died I was at work at the newspaper.
There was nothing for me to do but what I did,
which was answer the phone when the call came in,
and listen to sobswallowed words
and authentic
left-hooked pain
that couldn't touch the dancing me
over the wires.

I stood up and told my editor Mitch I was leaving
for my father was dead
and there were things
that needed my attention.
He nodded.

I went back to my desk
and finished typing up
a brief about a house fire,
suspected arson,
in the Queensborough neighborhood.

Firefighters had arrived to find the house completely engulfed in flames.

When I got in my car and turned the key,
the radio blared on big rock music
1980s hairpop
from some Hollywood spandex band
and I thought
"Why not?"
"Why shouldn't it?"
"Why is the world not rent? Why is the sun
so warm
and purifying?"

I put my arm around my mother.
It was an act of volition,
something I decided to do.
Something like a platitude
or something I would have been embarrassed
not to have done
had anyone
been looking.

They were all weeping
in the decorous, quiet way
our people have
of crying
like our hearts are hurting us.

It is not our hearts that hurt.
The pain—if we feel it—isn't
located in our breasts but
behind the eyes perhaps
or else grief is glandular,
an inner wash,
an acid bath eating
away the idol
(shiny and careworn)
we have made of our longings
and our wishful
sideways apprehensions
of ourselves.

My father was the one I came here to replace
and his dying young was not designed
to make me feel guilt
or even fear my own
inevitable
stopping
burning out
or what have you.

He was in ways finer than I am
and in other ways not so fine
but I am not here to resent him
or to carry on in a way
I might imagine would make
him proud
if he could only see me now.

(And who knows? Perhaps he can.
I would not be so surprised;
though I believe it is human to doubt and
that only the brave, the true and the stupid
can believe the way
they say we all must.)

2.

There was an episode in a funeral home
where my father's body lay
face up and cold
his thin hair combed, Vitalis-ed
and
his eyes pressed shut.

(I kissed his forehead. It was cool and smooth as marble.)

There were people
hundreds, I guess,
who knew him and who
bothered to come by although
I didn't recognize many of them.

And I felt like
they were stealing
something I never
really had anyway.
Something like
the connectedness
we are supposed to feel
with those people we are born to,
whose codes we learn
—whose hypocrisies we cherish—
whose transparencies we accept
and whose nimble mysteries eventually
become nothing more or less
than the occasion for a tight
begrudging smile.

An old black gentleman,
whom I had never met before,
took my hand and pumped it
saying
"You must be the son.
You must be the son.
I loved.
I loved your father."

There were tears gleaming platinum
on his creased and weary face.

There was a card from Mickey Mantle
tented on the bar
in the dark room
in which my father
used to drink and
watch his baseball
before he went into the hospital
for those months of chemo
and pity
and the shame of
wasting down.

Someone said the suffering was over
and I wanted
to bust them in the face
because I was that kind of face-busting boy,
just then.

But I was not that kind of boy for long and so
I simply nodded and
poured myself
a long gold Scotch
and drove to my girlfriend's house
to try to get her
to sleep with me again
or maybe one last time because
after all
my father had just died and
it wasn't a good time to break up.

We went for a long drive
out past Haughton and by the racetrack
and I thought about driving into Texas
away from the overtaking night.

She said
she wouldn't come to the funeral
because all that death and dying stuff creeped her out.

3.

We went out on a July day
in red silk and blue wool
and put him in the ground
because
that is what you do.

We were dutiful and our sweat
tracked down like tears
and splattered fat
on the graveside dirt.

The city editor came and looked concerned and said
things softly to my mother
that caused her to nod.
I stared hard at the ground.

And if they thought anything
they thought that I was grieving.
And I was. Though
I still can't say today
for what or whom.

I just wish things could be different
that you could have hung around a while
that you could have made grandaddy
that you didn't have to puke and ache and fry
with the kind of fear I know the morphine
(or the hash that Billy brought you)
could not begin to cut.

I just wish I could believe in
all the soothing sounds and lowing
all the stories that we make up
so we don't have to feel so lonely
and so futile
and so numb.

I always kind of liked you, Dad,
and I understood
it wasn't easy with a kid like me,
so much like you but different.
I always thought you always
tried to do the best you could.

I remember the whiskey scrape
of your day-old beard
against my cheek and how you told me
some boxers could use their stubble
as an abrading weapon
in the clinches.
And
how you had one professional fight
and won it too
under an assumed name in Kansas City
the year before I was born
and that you had never told nobody
not even my mother
about it.

I'm older now than you were when you died.
And I don't know how you did it.
I know when the cancer comes to get me
I'll be so terrified.
I don't know what kept you from
screaming
and swearing
or dousing the blazing wick
with that black pistol
you kept in your desk drawer
for whatever eventuality,
for whatever monster,
ever broke into
your house,
our lives.

I wouldn't have held it against you.

Though I guess
I might have other worries
I don't have,
not at this moment, anyway.

There is no comfort but in Jesus
or in Allah
or in Buddha
or in Moses or whatever
shitlord
whose name
you want to take in vain

when you have
to look into the faces
of the pity-givers and the bored.

I remember I brought you a contraband milkshake
from the Dairy Queen
and that we played gin rummy
until you were so tired
too tired
to keep it up.

You slept
and in the morning you were dead.

And I was at work.
You didn't have to worry.
I always worked hard,
hard as you,
and now
I've found a family.
I know how things are.
I see you in mirrors
and I hear you
breathing;
your cigarette a redthrob beacon
glowing in the dankdark
caverns of my multi-chambered
heart.

# THOMAS CHATTERTON

(rockabilly)


For Bill Jones


Standing in the door
don't turn your back on me.
I get sorta bored
with all this and leather and lethargy.
I don't like to be ignored
I don't like how you talk to me.

You don't want to dance,
you just want someone to take you home.
I've got less of a chance
than a hippie in the ThunderDome.

Hanging in the hall
with the priest and your arch-enemies,
drinking grain alcohol,
and spouting New Age heresies.
I see you leaning 'ginst the wall
while they're burning me in effigy.

The worst sin is to be dull,
keep it less than three minutes long,
light as a serpent's skull,
opaque as a John-Taupin song.

You got sex on your breath
and murder in your heart for me,
you got left bereft,
and when I took my vow of chastity
now you ain't got nothing left,
not a modicum of dignity.

I'm a handsome guy
though they say that looks don't matter none.
I can always get by
because I look like Thomas Chatterton.

Reading lyric sheets
never trusting what you hear.
Was it Yeats or was it Keats
who bit your little bitty pretty ear?
Oh, you only read the Beats
and a little bit of Norman Lear?

*Deus absconditus*
I can't sing but I can scream.
The devil does entreat us
to suffer for his teenage dream.

You got a boarding pass
they're counting down to ecstasy.
Raise your empty glass
to the mess the jackals made of me.
Like a whore-monger at mass
I'm dripping with hypocrisy.

I don't like to lie
and I don't want you to be misled.
I'm not afraid to die
but I'm scared to death of being dead.

# DISAPPEARING REMBRANDTS

There are tests we can run on the canvas
to ensure authenticity.
We carbon date hallucinations
from the seventeenth century.
To the master, to the student,
we assign the catalogue.
Without favor, with precision,
like a laser cuts through fog.

Sometimes an unsteady brushstroke,
perhaps an eyelash rendered queer,
or if proportion slips and struggles,
we'll bring our quiet science to bear.
Seven hundred and fifty imposters
debunked and reclassified,
serve to certify our connoisseurship
as we conquer, and divide.

Baubles bounce on gathered velvet,
they twist and shimmer in the sun.
Where paint's applied and light's reflected
the human eye can be undone.
Signature? A tidy little monster.
Competence? A crafty liar.
This one here's worth sixty million,
fling that one into the fire.

Rembrandt was a wily rascal,
who produced great works of genius
but he had pupils not so clever
and he gave work to Fabritius.
So we unlock the bliss and thunder
with our scholarship and chemicals.
We explode the awe and wonder
of the myth of miracles.

# Poems for Sale

I bought this poem on Fourteenth Street
between avenues Second and Third
from an ironic kid who dressed like a beat
and whose hands fluttered like a bird
over the keys of an Underwood
or a Selectric IBM
while the boys and girls of NYU
stepped around—or right over—him.

Ripping pecked-up pages from his machine
and banging the carriage return,
he sat like a monk doused with gasoline,
willing his chakra to burn.

He wore a Salvation Army sports coat,
a shirt as pale as an angel's lie,
a pork pie hat; and looped 'round his throat,
an Allen Ginsberg tie.
Blood tangled and pooled in his eyewhites.
He breathed absinthe and nicotine.
His hair was streaked with blond highlights.
His fingernails? Ragged, but clean.

He asked for ten dollars, I offered five;
we settled on six and shook hands,
on a few fuzzy stanzas of iambic jive
no one left on earth understands.

I smuggled this contraband onto the plane,
taped to the inside of my thigh.
It burned like a bitch but I withstood the pain
and carried the poetry on high.
Now I've just pulled it out and I've read it through
and I'm wondering if it's any good.
It's just black glyphs on paper. What can you do?
I think maybe he sold me a dud.

# CANADIANS

Karen told her friend Bob from Ontario
that all Canadians were sweet
but people from Vancouver
tended to be a little nicer
than people from
Toronto.

Bob said:
"Well, fuck you then."

# GOING TO THE BOATS

(telecaster through vibrolux)

I dreamt
I was nearly hit by lightning.
I was working on the truck
and it began to rain
smeltgray
and I felt the ozone fizz
and I backed off just
as it bluebolted
the engine block. Powee.

It woke me up.
So I went out back and peed
and looked up at the gleeful moon
and felt the luck (and need)
heartcharging through my body.

So I went to the ATM and took
two hundred dollars only
from out the joint account.

I stuck those ten crisp twenties
in my wallet
with all the limpworn ones and fives
I've grown to take for granted
and spend with something like impunity
despite the debts
we owe on paper to some Wisconsin company.

I drove to Shreveport in the middle of the night
and walked out on the water
into the electronic jing and mineral clatter
(where money meets its anti-matter)
of the circus throb casino.

Poker is more skill than chance
but I felt the quiver,
the magic dance
and shiver,
as the killing floor
rocked on the river.
I won.

And then,
I lost and felt
the bitterness descend:
That I was me and they were they
and I was at their table, in the end,
not as their guest, but as their prey.

And there is exhilaration
in being sucked out
and fucked up,
in drinking free cheap whiskey
from a plastic cup.

It is, after all, something to do.

There is recompense in losing
if you can stand it like a man.
Let the match burn to your fingertips,
let the flesh smart
and the mortification thrill you.

You grow to like feeling
 scraped out and empty,
a pacing wolf
in your gut,
the peaceless satisfaction
of having found your level.

I groped homeward drunk,
their lessons stinging in my cheek,
reprimanded, mild and meek.

Don't tell me about the meritocracy.
I just don't see it. It's not there to see.
There's rich folks and there're folks like you and me
to grease the gears of the economy.
I won't apologize for being me.
Not to you or to those in the city
who run the banks and credit companies.
I'll pay it back; just sayin' don't push me.

The world is rigged up like a carny game.
You might win shit but it's shit all the same.
They say that college counts and it does some
but not as much as your grandfather's name.
So the only chance you have is to play
this prepared game in the way that they say
or maybe save your paycheck for the day
some angel comes to bear your ass away.

# Matty Alou

No one remembers much
beyond the obvious
like Pete Rose crashing into poor Ray Fosse
or where they were when JFK
was shot.

So why it is
I close my eyes today
and see a flash of black and gold
across a green field
I cannot say.

You had four hits in four at bats
though Fergie Jenkins won the game—
his twentieth of 1968,
the year before the Cubs' collapse.
It was on a Saturday.

Wrigley Field. 28 September.
Si, Mateo. I remember.

# Boozy Musings of Defeated Deemed Extraneous

I went out on election night,
after the TV stations had called it
and I had interviewed the bright young hope,
to the house of the old pol.
A loser
whose name has fled—Carroll, he was called—
the nation of my mind
for Nambian exile.

His wife led me in
to his dim gold den
with the cherrywood chairs
and the Scotch in highball glasses,
heavy as revolvers.

"It is hard to lose
especially when
you thought they liked you
and were grateful for your
years of service. You will
have a drink, son?"

(I did because back then
that was how those things were done.
It isn't like it is now.
Drinking on the job
is a fireable offense
and you can't
take whiskey from a source.)

"They can go to hell for all I care.
I did my best for them and they
turn around and vote
for the facile and broadshouldered,
the pleasant and the good.
It doesn't work like that
they'll see; and all their charming lads
will come to grief.
It takes
a man like me.
Rude and cunning,
half a liar,

half a thief."
I wrote this down
and wrote it up,
inverted pyramid style.
An editor took the top four inches—
the frothy head—
and left the rest to die
in the gutter of the composing table.

This unquoted man whose name I cannot quite recall
died weeks later behind the wheel
of his parked Cadillac.
His outvoted heart gave out, that's all,
something in his viscera—wind and reel—
sparked an attack.

It would be speculative to say,
we killed him with our unattentiveness.
But when I pray
I pray for losers,
for the stand-up guys in movies
who never get the girl
but show up anyway
at the wedding bearing
good wishes
and forgiveness
wrapped in smallpox blankets.

# ON BEING CALLED "RACIST" IN THE NEWSPAPER

In his letter to the editor
the professor makes good points about
how The South, if it ever was, is not
extant. And should never rise again.
Not even in my romantic heart.

Because I never picked any cotton
(though my momma did, and my daddy
died young; a-working for the Air Force),
and my career in tobacco was
cut short by my colorblindedness.
And the only blues I ever played
was ersatz, whiteboy, E-A-B stuff,
twelve bars below the Texas Street bridge.

Still I don't think he meant to be rude;
to challenge the authenticity
of my experience or to say
that identity is just a mask
that may be slipped on or off at will.

He knows as well as I that there is
bigotry in the white trash blood
that laps in my breast and collects hot
in my pink ears whenever I am
called to task by the righteous victims
of pharaoh's unjust and merciless,
reckless and punishing hatefulness.

Some of my ancestors were busthead
imbibers, bad debtors and horse thieves.
Some of them were ignorant and mean.
And had I been of their time then
I probably would have been like them.

Yet might I respectfully submit
that the professor is incorrect;
Jack Cash was no apologist, sir.
Not for the louts and the deniers.
They silklynched him in Mexico,
for telling truths. Sure as Trotsky was
assassinated, they came for him
in their ghost hoods with tar and pitch.
Like Wolfe said, you can't go home again.

I disagree with his contention
that Welty and O'Connor were "mere
sentimentalists" who sought to make
that South—which has never existed—
"more palatable" to callow minds.
Should we just agree to disagree?

I never meant to suggest the world
is less cruel or brutish than it is
or that I could ever feel your pain
or guess at the hurt and shame you knew
and still know in your capacity
as the official arbiter of taste
and seemliness in matters of race
and whom may get into whose face.
So I offer this apology.

For every word you misunderstood,
and for every dumbass peckerwood
whoever mumbled "Fergit Hell"
or raised a rebel flag or rebel yell.
You look at me and see those boys?

Well, I do too and I am not proud
of what they do and what we've allowed.
But you do not know me, sir, at all.
Still you presume, and you pretend
I would not have you for a friend.
And I might not; for I hold grudges.
But it is history that judges.

# ELLIS ISLAND

We came on a boat
heavy with foreigners
across the tea-stained harbor
on a brilliant September day

the Japanese man on the ferry
wore a shirt with the words
"Trendy Friend Club"
and carried a Nikon camera

"People sometimes make their own stereotypes," you said
because no American would wear
a shirt so tight
as the Italian
(and what was with
the four-inch numerals on the breast?
it had to be a soccer football thing)

your grandfather Nicolai's name
was not in the computer system
and that was disappointing
for I'd have liked to see his passport photograph
and matched his calibrated Croat gaze
to yours

Yanko, your father,
says Nicolai brought a wife with him
and when she died
he went back to Zagreb
and married another
and when she died
he did it again

the last one was Yanko's mother
your grandmother

in those days, I guess
you brought over what you could
and if you could afford to ferry back
and save another
that was just what you did
no question about it
the new world was a better world
there was no question then

Yanko went to school with Jesse Owens
and lost his Croatian long ago
he grew up American tall and square
and was a corpsman
in The War

we took it all down on microcassette, remember?
the day we drove to Amish country
you interviewed him and he told stories
you had never heard before
about his brothers
George and Mike and little Nick
and poker games
in the Philippines

the past is a foreign country from which we are exiled
and from which we exile ourselves
its customs and language are strange
we are *émigrés* from its storied pomp
but for it our bones yearn

# STAND MY GROUND

(a protest song in D)

You think you know my story,
You saw it on the MSNBC.
Things might have turned out different,
if they'd let me in that damn academy.
But I ain't a good test taker,
I guess I got a little A.D.D.
(Kids, don't burn that marijuana
It messes with your short term memory.)

Now Tom Cotton, he was sayin'
how they can use their food stamps to buy steak.
And Obama gives 'em iPhones,
while the working man just can't catch a break.
Sometimes I get so angry,
listening to Rush Limbaugh that I shake.
But I didn't do no felony:
Maybe I just made a sad mistake.

They gave me back my pistol,
my black Kel-Tec PF-9
I ain't James Franco in Spring Breakers
But I'm proud to call the little honey mine.
You know he was a total stranger
I'd never before seen him hanging 'round
I never saw what hit me
But I know I've got a right to stand my ground.

Like I told the operator
He looked like he's about to B&E
He was cutting through the houses
And he walking a little bit too leisurely
I got on the radio, they asked his 20
And so I got out to see
When he weaponized that sidewalk
I swear I thought that it was either him or me.

I can prove that I'm not racist
I even took a black girl to the prom
It don't matter to Al Sharpton
But I don't give a rat's ass where you're from
There's people who belong here

And people who just want to take your stuff
You've got your punkish element
And guys like me who've finally had enough.

Maybe Tray was in the wrong place
I know I'd never even heard his name
It was hard to tell with that hoodie
But I think he looked a little like The Game
I know I have a right to be here
And there's a reason that we live behind these gates
I know that fear is the great corrosive
And that he is lost who hesitates.

You know he was a total stranger
I'd never before seen him hanging 'round
I never saw what hit me
But I know I've got a right to stand my ground.

# WAT PROMKUNARAM

*"Your honor, in June of 1991, Jonathan Doody and I got together and planned to rob and burglarize the Thai Buddhist temple. Part of our plan was to leave no witnesses. On the evening of August 9th 1991, we started to put our plan in action. Jonathan and I drove to the temple. I was armed with a 20-gauge pump shotgun. Jonathan was armed with a .22-caliber semiautomatic rifle . . . Before leaving the temple, Jonathan told me, 'No witnesses.' I told him 'Robbery is one thing, but murder is another.' Jonathan repeated to me that there could be no witnesses. He then stepped to my right and, while armed with the .22-caliber rifle, began shooting the nine occupants while they were laying on the floor. I began firing my 20 gauge shotgun, but fired not to kill anyone. I fired four rounds from my shotgun toward the nine people laying on the floor."*

—Alex Garcia, statement to Judge Gregory Martin upon pleading guilty to murder.

The one called Boy
—Chirapong—drew orange-red
his unfiltered Camel cigarette
and looked east over the valley
to the incandescent urban hum
beneath the glistening stars.

He could feel August stinging
through his sandals.
The desert dryheat
drifting skyward
like the prayers
of monks and nuns.

His aunt had sent him
to Arizona
to get him out of trouble
to get him out of Bangkok.
He had no truck
with the superstitions, the dharma or his uncle the abbot's politics.

He wanted only
Arizona
and what lay beyond, the Burger Kings

and *farang* girls
with rice milk titties.

He wanted money of his own
and to ride like Kerouac
with a nightshining heart and second language English
on his tongue.
He had two thousand dollars
and long black hair like a bargirl's
and a plastic
*Terminator 2* cup
from Subway.

2.

There was an American kid
tucked up like the dwarf in a Mechanical Turk
in Jonathan Doody.

He was not his Asiatic face
or the dandruff
that was brushed
from his Air Force Junior ROTC uniform
by the Colonel at inspection.

("Get yourself some Head and Shoulders, son," he said.)

He had been to Germany
and watched Phantoms and Vipers
rock and curl in the sky
and experienced an intimation
of how it was to be
for him.

Jonathan was Steve Canyon
done up
in Dragon Lady drag
and the cheerleaders
would recognize
when he completed his secret mission
and drove his hot Camaro

into the lot
of Agua Fria High School.

"Football is for rednecks,"
he told Handsome Alex
and the two of them went
into the desert
to shoot cans.

They went into the White Tank Mountains
to invent a silencer.

3.

Matthew Miller
came to the temple
curious about the culture.
He wanted to perfect his Thai,
the language of grandmother Foi
and his mother Fong.

At sixteen
part of him regretted the tattoos and the pot,
the slovenly days.
And part of him felt
reprimanded.

Part of him felt
sanctified,
prepared for some obscure purpose
to be revealed to him
at some future time.

"Good"
was how he felt.


"Mr. GQ"
they called him for
the thrift store suits

he cleaned and pressed
and wore to school.

He was sixteen
and played guitar
and came
to be an acolyte
the day David Doody
left the Wat.

4.

David told Jonathan
There was money
in that temple:
more than what the congregation
pinned on trees
in the sanctuary.

More than what was in their wallets,
more than Boy
kept in his room.
Maybe laundered poppy funds from Chiang Mai
near Burma
and a safe too.

It was just kid talk—
not the sort of thing
anyone takes seriously.

5.

What Jonathan hated
was the Otherness forcing
its way through his being
snarling the tongue
that would speak
no more Thai forever.

What Jonathan hated
was the orange and saffron
the chanting and the way

the robes bared
the womanish shoulders
of the monks.
What Jonathan hated
was the punkass AM Posse
that hung around the Whataburger
with their big talk
and no action.

What Jonathan hated
was stasis and
the small hard nub
of self
he felt pressing in his chest.


*Mind is the forerunner of (all evil) states. Mind is chief. Mind-made they are.*


What Jonathan hated
was the pipsqueaky ennui
the infirm, out-of-register
reflection he caught
in the contemplative
cow-eyed, slim-smiling
faces of the Buddha boys.

What Jonathan hated
was sacking groceries
in the commissary
with an IQ of 134.

6.

It was a game
they called
an "intrusion alert exercise."
Jonathan and Alex
kitted themselves out
in BDUs
(Battle Dress Uniforms)
with silk scarves
over their mouths

and bad-looking snow boots
they bought at the BX.

They took the guns and knives
and went with G_ and R_
into the scrub,
past the floodlights
throwing shadows,
into the sanctuary
past the collection boxes
stuffed with bills.
Maybe they overlooked them
or maybe they figured collection offerings
were but
chump change
compared to
what was in the safe they never opened
or the "chest full of money"
Jonathan said was there.

7.

Matthew Miller and Boy knew Jonathan
and maybe Alex too
and maybe the others.

Jonathan said (allegedly)
they could not let them live.

Jonathan said (allegedly)
that once you've shot
someone mercenary style
you never forget the sight
or the sound
as blood jets
and bubbles
from the little hole
punched in the head.

8.

The *Dhammapada* says:

*Hatred is never appeased by hatred.*

*Hatred is appeased by nonhatred.*
*That is the eternal law.*

9.

The next morning
Chawnee came to the temple
with breakfast for the monks.
She was annoyed to see
the sprinklers
snapping
in the yard.
10.

Before the football game
police came for Jonathan.

He was in his Color Guard uniform
with the dummy rifle painted white.
His chromed helmet
splintering the stadium lights,
dazzling the crowd.

"Take it off, son,"
said the detective
who laid his hands
on  Jonathan's head
to guide him gently
into the back seat
of the patrol car.

# FILM AND MUSIC

*For Ray McKinnon*

I want to make a film
because it is always better to show than tell
because the heart is inarticulate
a method mumbler.

I want frame after frame
a perfect lightshot universe.


Or maybe
I should dispense with language altogether
and make music
an oscillating jazz of
blue codes
pinned to a warped and spinning mandala.

But when I was in a band
a communion unfolded
in which I could not share.

The others smiled at me
but knew
that when the bass came round
with its syrupy questions
I had no answer.

I watched their hands sometimes
and did the math
and came in on the backside of the beat
but it was work for me
and only joy sporadically.

They were kind to the outsider
but it always hard to learn
that what you believe yourself to love
is impossible to earn.

So I am back to solitary rhythms,
these taps and clacks,
and the filling up of whitespace
with spindly glyphs
and spider tracks.

And thinking of Fellini
in the Deep South
and focus pullers
and the legions you command
to make a moment.

I want to make a film
but I want to make it by myself
to cast it from sleep-dragged memories.
driftwood nostalgia,
and furnish it with pale yellow light
and brownblack shadows.

I want fluency in different tongues.
I want guidance and direction.
I want to breathe into my lungs
that sharp air of connection.

# SEEDTICK ROAD

*For Paul Bowen*

Today an American journalist
told me proudly she had (nicely) asked
Catherine Deneuve, in an interview,
to please extinguish her cigarette.
Because here we have a democracy
and we have a right not to be vexed
by snooty foreign former sex kittens
who can't read the posted "No Smoking" signs.

Deneuve stubbed it out but was not happy.
"You Americans think you make the rules."
Yes, ma'am, sometimes we do. That is the way
we do things here. Someone has to be in charge.
And it might as well be the US of A.
(Or as my old baseball coach used to say:
"Smoke a Gauloise in hell, goddamn Frenchy.")

Well, how about that? You really told her.
And she told you back, but don't feel too bad.
I might prefer cigarettes to tension
but I ask to sleep in non-smoking rooms
and I don't eat the cookies some bring to work.
I like gyms and the lactic acid wash
in my limbs that comes from lifting barbells.
In principal, I am a Puritan.

Yet everything we do serves to erase
a bit more of this thing we know as "I"
Experience decimates our race
and even the non-smokers have to die.

I did not say this to her. I nodded
and looked back down at my laptop screen.
I can be bad that way, a "no-talker"
as they used to say on Jerry Seinfeld.
But I have decided to do better.
So I told her I never smoked, not really,
though when I played guitar sometimes in bands
I'd stick a cigarette in the corner
of my mouth and make a Keith Richard sneer.
"Did you sing too?" Not too much. A little.

I said, smokers always hate me for it,
but I never had a jones for nicotine.
I'd smoke onstage—half a pack a week—
yet I'd never think of them otherwise.
It isn't fair. I should have some karmic debt.
My grandfather had a tobacco farm
outside Pembroke, Georgia, near Savannah.
I suppose it was small as those things go
But he made a good living and raised up
five sons and four daughters on Seedtick Road.

Like all the old tobacco men he smoked.
He lost a lung but never even tried to quit
and died when he was sixty-three or four.
And after his death his sons sold away
an acre here and there and let the fields
go fallow for the want of industry.
They married young and hauled in house trailers
and squatted on the land. It was still theirs
by law. But even as I child I saw
how provisional and tawdry it seemed.
I should remember more. I don't; it's hard
for me to believe as a boy of nine
I'd walk the fields and stand in the dim cool
fragrant vault of silverwood curing barns.

But I did, and I drove the tractor too.
A blue Ford, with a naked metal seat.
My Uncle Mike taught me to drive it—
a gesture of reconciliation
after a fistfight, so I wouldn't tell.
I wouldn't have anyway, I never did.
He was just eighteen months older than me
but he had a gun and a motorbike
while I collected baseball cards and read
Richard Henry Dana, John R. Tunis
and Stephen Meador's books on the front porch.

My grandmother lived on Seedtick Road
for seventy-five years. It was unpaved
and I believe it's still a dirt road today.
I took my wife there once a few years ago.
There was a party for my grandmother.
She was in her mid-ninties at the time.
Everyone thought it'd be her last Christmas,
so we rode out with mother after dark.

Though it had been nearly thirty-five years
since I'd been down that road I recognized
the turnoff and the black trees bearing moss.
I felt a cold clutch in my faithless heart
—a traitor trundled home in heavy chains.

There was a crowd at granny's new brick house
(long claimed by weeds, the old place down the road)
her kitchen was thick with the smoky smell
of sliced peaches, gravy and Virginia Slims.
My uncles were all old; so were my aunts,
they sipped sweet iced tea because they were off
the booze now—"thank you, Jesus Christ, my lord."
They hugged my neck and whispered in my ear
and took Karen by the hand to show her
the photographs of couples in the hall.
(My Aunt Patricia told her that sometimes
after someone got divorced or broke up
she'd sneak in and take down the ex's picture.)

They were glad to see us but no one asked
much about our lives, only if we were
happy. We told them we were then went out
into the backyard to breathe and look up
at the silver-peppered country night sky.

Across the gray lawn, I saw a red tip,
a cigarette glowing, near the back door
of Roy's—my hermit uncle's—mobile home.
A signal. A green glow from Daisy's dock.
His way of telling us, he's still alive.

www.ingramcontent.com/pod-product-compliance
Lightning Source LLC
LaVergne TN
LVHW051347080426
835509LV00020BA/3320